YOUR KNOWLEDGE HAS VALUE

Felix Ale

A critial review about "The Divine Matrix" by Gregg Braden

GRIN Publishing

Bibliographic information published by the German National Library:

The German National Library lists this publication in the National Bibliography; detailed bibliographic data are available on the Internet at http://dnb.dnb.de .

Imprint:

Copyright © 2014 GRIN Verlag GmbH
Print and binding: Books on Demand GmbH, Norderstedt Germany
ISBN: 978-3-656-89263-2

This book at GRIN:

http://www.grin.com/en/e-book/289011/a-critial-review-about-the-divine-matrix-by-gregg-braden

GRIN - Your knowledge has value

Since its foundation in 1998, GRIN has specialized in publishing academic texts by students, college teachers and other academics as e-book and printed book. The website www.grin.com is an ideal platform for presenting term papers, final papers, scientific essays, dissertations and specialist books.

Visit us on the internet:

http://www.grin.com/

http://www.facebook.com/grincom

http://www.twitter.com/grin_com

ALE FELIX BABATUNDE

COURSE TITLE:
THE DIVINE MATRIX-A CRITICAL REVIEW

SCHOOL OF SOCIAL AND HUMAN STUDIES
MAJOR:PhD JOURNALISM
ATLANTIC INTERNATIONAL UNIVERSITY.

SUBMMITED – 10THDECEMBER,2014.

Book Review: The Divine Matrix by Gregg Braden

The debate on the origin of man, the universe and everything in it both tangible and intangible has been raging for many years. On one side of the debate, since time immemorial, is the church and the other side are the scientists. The church and the scientists have vehemently opposed each other's ideologies and explanations. At the height of the opposition from the church was the Dark Age; an era remembered for the high handed tactics used by the church to silence the scientists. The persecutions and the ban on the public or private discussion of scientific knowledge were widespread. Opposing the church's position on the origin of earth was considered the origin of sin; an abomination punishable by death. Despite these oppositions, the scientists managed to hold their own ground secretly dispensing their ideas to the world. Theories have been formulated while many scholars, scientists and theologians alike, have written countless papers, each pressing for the truth from their own perspective. For the religious scientists especially physicists and some liberal churches and clergymen the lack of concession has always provided a window of opportunity to find the scientific evidence with a common view. But like old times, their ideologies, explanations and experiments have been met with skepticism. Therefore, it is always an overwhelming experience to find an objective voice in tackling the question of the origin of the earth and everything.

Gregg Braden's book, *The Divine Matrix* that seeks to justify and offer meaning to the origin of both the tangible and intangible things of the universe offers one of the most elusive and divisive evidence. The origin of the web of energy in the universe has for many years been a bone of contention between the church and science. From the time of Galileo to the modern times marked with technological advancements to carry out research, humanity has failed spectacularly to comprehensively and neutrally define their origin and everything around them. It is this knowledge gap that Braden aims at plugging and bridging. Braden aims at offering an olive branch through which both divides of the debate can reach out to each other and understanding life happenings and the interconnections between everything in the human life. Going through the book, one cannot fail to feel the transformative power of the knowledge that Braden has one on a controversial topic. It is a journey that Braden proudly takes his audience. It is a journey whose ultimate end is to bridge the gap between spirituality and science. The extraordinary, based on evidence from scientific experiments, ends in The Divine Matrix; the ultimate answer to understanding miracles, emotions, sufferings and the force that links all creations in the universe.

Miracles as fronted by our religions are one of the central dogmas of Christianity and other faiths. It requires absolute faith to believe in miracles. Many people sometimes find it difficult to believe some of events that would basically be regarded as miracles by religious zealots. The early scientists usually find themselves testing the rationality of events around them that would pass for miracles. Believing with questioning; the absolute faith as we are taught by religion is not one of their strongest points. They believe that, the seed of curiosity and inquisitiveness is sowed in children by the environment they interact with and especially the education system.

The fundamental questions that some scientists seek to find answers to everyday: at what point does the intangible and tangible interact? What is the connection between reality and our imagination as Christians? Can modern Christians identify with the covenants, miracles and sufferings within the context of science? How can we address and understand the Christian dogmas in spite of the advancements and permeation of scientific knowledge? To what extent can Christians identify with scientific knowledge with religious connotations? Are miracles and understanding of the origin of the universe relevant in a modern day world marred in skepticism and glorification of rationality and scientific evidence as the bearer of the absolute truth? When contextualized, to some scientists, the answers to these questions reveal if Jesus

Christ fulfills Israel's destiny and if the church is heir to Israel's mission. The answers to these questions will therefore make Israel's history our history, Israel's call our call and Israel's old covenant the pattern for our new covenant. But most significantly, these answers would become part of the many scientific-based approaches to religion that would mark the beginning of the end of the conflict between religion and science. It would mark an end to the stranglehold of the population's mind by both sides when it comes to understanding religion.

The overriding belief within the Christian circles, a belief that I also share, is that God created man and all other living things plus the earth as clearly outlined in the book of Genesis. Moreover, the Christians, who represent a huge portion of the world's population, believe that as stated in the Bible that everything that God created was perfect. These were views and beliefs that have been religiously and ritually followed and believed for many years without being questioned. They have become conventional and traditional explanations used by all and sundry to explain every phenomenon in the universe. During the early era, this was done out of fear of sabotaging the church which had political, social and economic authority. It became a taboo to question the existence of creation as this would ultimately raise doubts about the existence of God Himself. This would be tantamount to treason; a heinous crime that many had lost their lives for. The status quo was preserved and perpetuated by both the church and the public in general. Even today, many individuals despite their religious inclination believe some of these ideologies.

However, the popularity of science during the early ages and even today gave birth to hard line beliefs that have slowly being challenging the church's position on the existence of the universe. Indeed, radical scientific views have directly attacked the very existence of God and ultimately stifled the Christians' views on creation. Rationality has, in many occasions, won some people over when it comes to understanding nature. The logical and plausible that science offers using scientific jargons has seen many people give a wide berth to some of the explanations put forth by religion with regards to the universe.

Reading Braden's book, I felt that Braden did not want to subjectively waddle into this old age debate. He does not intend to contradict neither the scientific nor the religious views on the matter. Rather, through real life events and scientific research from respected scientists to find a middle ground in ongoing debate. He lets scientists understand miracles and The Divine Matrix within the context of science and biblical teachings. To the Christians, the seamless marriage between science and religion in understanding the universe as ordained by Braden has a religious appeal.

Braden's assertion that tangible and intangible systems have a complex interlinking is a concept that I have come to appreciate over the years. It is a commonly applied business model that informs modern day business strategies. However, having it put in a layman's language using examples that I can easily relate to make it even clearer. It transforms the idea of interlinking of human lives and events from being mere ideologies, models and imaginations to real life events which are applicable in our everyday's life. Such understanding is born out of my new understanding that we have a common origin. That is, despite our glaring differences, we came from a single source: The Divine Matrix. Our emotions, sufferings and destinies despite their uniqueness are interlinked as they operate within a web of energy emanating from a central point.

Essentially what Braden is proposing is a paradigm shift from hard line Christianity and science which have polarized our societies. He puts the process of creation squarely in the hands of nature and its forces. However, such power emanates from central point that connects all creations and even all the abstract forms. The innumerable life forms are connected by the missing link which Braden has found. With the book, the concept of the universality of love is better understood. Braden's assertion that The Divine Matrix is the center of the existence of the universe enables me to form deeper understanding of people and things around me including the environment. I have learned to be more appreciative of the environment within which I stay knowing very well that we are interlinked; we have what many scientists termed as common origin. By reading the book, I now better understand the concept of Mother Nature. The book also offers a great insight into the constant calls that have been echoed around the world to preserve and conserve our environment: because there is an interlinking that sustains life in the universe. Our very existence is reliant on our ability to maintain the balance of the integrity and energy within the matrix.

The ground breaking scientific experiments especially those dealing with quantum physics also helped in developing a strong appreciation for imagination. Braden shows that every imagined thought and dream can be changed into reality through action. I am now more convinced that any conceivable thought can be put into action and that every dream is valid. Braden transforms dreams from illusions to reality giving me countless opportunities and ideas which I can put into reality. The book has helped in developing my self belief. I now understand that miracles are a reality; possibilities which we can realize, see and understand if we can contextualize them within the realm of the matrix. They become reality if we can understand that everything has an origin: the matrix. By understanding the importance of the matrix, it is indeed possible to create a bridge between our imaginations and beliefs. Imaginations can transform into actionable ideas and realities with appreciation of the matrix.

What also stands out from the book that helps in building self confidence and help in self determination is the ability of Braden to convince the readers that indeed they have the power to directly connect with the matrix and direct our world in our own way. This assurance created a special feeling in me especially when it comes to understanding puzzling concepts such as pain and suffering which usually confuse me. Pain and suffering are concepts that I believe most people including scientists and religious individuals have sadly failed to understand. Knowing that we can control sufferings by connecting with The Divine Matrix I believe can help in overcoming those emotionally taxing moments. It is a welcome relief for Braden to reassure the readers that we can actually create such positive feelings as joy and happiness. He holds that we can speak directly to the matrix by actions. The idea of positive or negative energy that we send to the universe has for sometime now been used by astronomers to explain daily occurrences in our lives including successes, failures and emotional statuses. However, having such information reinforced with real life and scientific evidences goes a long way in making the concept very relevant and easy to relate with.

The book is quite empowering and liberating. Knowing that I can unleash the power within me and actualize my dreams is a welcome in world bogged down by a myriad challenges. Knowing that I can channel and rearrange these seemingly conflicting ideologies and energies positively is very empowering. It acts as a pressure outlet and offers hope that things can get better if we make the connection with our inner self, the matrix and develop positive thoughts and energy around us. Understanding that the universe is a maze of interlinked energies that need to work synergistically to create a perfect balance is very liberating. This is because we are able to understand how the universe operates and how we can fit into the greater matrix. It bears open the DNA of life that many scientists and religious entities have for many years endeavored tried to attain with little success.

In conclusion, the debate on the origin of the universe between science and religion has always played out subjectively. Without a neutral or objective voice, it has always turned into a supremacy battle between science and religion. While the church had its way during the early eras, science's voice on the debate has increased exponentially almost lulling the church's voice. As someone with scientific background, Gregg Braden sets out to bend the two voices towards each and finds a neutral ground where the two can come to an understanding: the Divine Matrix. The book acknowledges and explains, in a layman's language, the connection between all elements of the universe. But most importantly, the book liberates and empowers the readers to take charge of their lives. It enables the reader to find grounds to understand miracles, imagination, reality and dreams within the context of both spirituality and science. The book enabled me to develop stronger bonds not only with my environment but also with my inner self. Knowing that I can control my emotions and environment is quite empowering and reassuring. It is an incredulous journey that have turned my dreams into reality and putting the controls of my emotions and relationships in my hand.

Reference

Braden, G. (2008). *The Devine Matrix: Bridging Time, Space, Miracles and Belief*. Hay House.